Tracking Trash

Flotsam, Jetsam, and the Science of Ocean Motion

To Mr. James Micarelli,

teacher of science and other truly important things

www.houghtonmifflinbooks.com

Book design by YAY! Design
The text of this book is set in Latienne.

A list of photo credits appears on page 55.
Maps by Jerry Malone

Library of Congress Cataloging-in-Publication Data

Burns, Loree Griffin.
Tracking trash : flotsam, jetsam, and the science of ocean motion / by Loree Griffin Burns.
    p. cm.
ISBN-13: 978-0-618-58131-3 (hardcover)
ISBN-10: 0-618-58131-6 (hardcover)
    1. Ocean currents—Juvenile literature.
    2. Marine debris—Juvenile literature.
    I. Title.

GC232.B87 2007
551.46'2—dc22

2006011534

Printed in Singapore
TWP 10 9 8 7 6 5 4 3 2 1

Loree Griffin Burns

Tracking Trash

Flotsam, Jetsam, and the Science of Ocean Motion

HOUGHTON MIFFLIN COMPANY. Boston 2007

Contents

*Debris from a shipwreck lies near
a patch of coral in the Pacific Ocean.*

CHAPTER ONE

A Spill of Opportunity

Benjamin Franklin, the famous inventor and patriot, was one of America's earliest ocean scientists. Although he eventually conducted experiments at sea, Franklin's early interest in the ocean stemmed from his job as deputy postmaster general of the American colonies. It was Franklin's duty to ensure that mail was carried between Europe and the colonies as efficiently as possible. While studying the fastest routes across the Atlantic Ocean, he talked to the captains of merchant vessels and whaling ships. From them he learned about a strange stream of seawater that flowed across the Atlantic, a virtual river in the middle of the sea.

The Franklin-Folger chart, published in 1769, shows the Gulf Stream as a dark river of seawater flowing west to east across the Atlantic Ocean.

1

According to these experienced sailors, this stream followed a distinct west-to-east path across the ocean and its movement could help or hinder sailing ships. Ships headed from America to Europe could travel much faster if they sailed within the stream. Ships sailing from Europe to America, on the other hand, could be delayed for weeks if they tried to sail against the stream's flow. Using this information, Franklin published the first map describing the so-called Gulf Stream in 1769. Its purpose was to improve the speed of mail, but Franklin's map also provided early evidence that ocean movement can have a large impact on human activities.

Though it was not clear in Franklin's day, distinct streams of seawater exist throughout the world ocean. Modern ocean scientists, or oceanographers, call these streams "currents," and we now know that they affect our world in ways that go far beyond the sailing of ships. For example, the location of ocean currents can dictate the climate of locations on land. Consider the fact that cities in Europe are much warmer than cities located at the same latitude on the opposite side of the Atlantic Ocean, in North America. Scientists believe the warm waters of the Gulf Stream heat the winds that, in turn, carry a pleasant climate to northern Europe. Another example of the impact ocean currents have on our world is the weather event known as El Niño. During El Niño, shifting wind patterns and ocean currents in and around the southern Pacific Ocean trigger changes in the local environment. These changes, which can include depleted fish populations and increased rainfall, have a large impact on the lives and livelihoods of the people who live in this area.

currents

climate

weather

environment

What forces drive the ocean currents? What boundaries, if any, guide their path through the ocean? Can understanding ocean currents help us to preserve the marine environment and the creatures that live in it? These are just a few of the questions that occupy the minds of modern-day oceanographers. Like Benjamin Franklin, these men and women are curious about the ocean; they hope their work, like his, will help us to understand one of our planet's most precious natural resources.

Dr. Curtis Ebbesmeyer shares these lofty goals, although his methods for understanding the ocean are, well, just a little unusual. First of all, Curt's experiments rely heavily on flotsam and jetsam, floating trash that falls or is thrown from ships at sea. Some of his most famous experiments involve sneakers and rubber ducks. What's more, Curt's assistants are a team of mostly amateur ocean observers located all over the globe. Nonetheless, Curt has made a name for himself in the oceanography world. He is widely considered to be the leading expert on flotsam and jetsam. The results of his work have been published in scientific journals. He speaks at conventions and gives interviews to television and radio reporters around the world. And every

From the natural "sea beans" on his favorite necklace to man-made plastic trash, Curt Ebbesmeyer is fascinated by how—and what— the ocean moves.

"Tracking toys and sneakers gives us a chance to see what the ocean does with our trash . . . and we can learn from it."

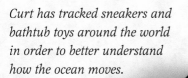

Curt has tracked sneakers and bathtub toys around the world in order to better understand how the ocean moves.

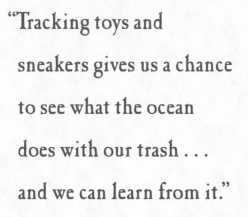

year he visits schools near his Seattle, Washington, home to tell children why his work is important.

"Tracking toys and sneakers gives us a chance to see what the ocean does with our trash," Curt says. "We can see the movement of trash by the great ocean currents and we can see the disintegration of the trash over time . . . and we can learn from it."

Curt didn't always track trash. His early work with ocean currents was quite ordinary.

If someone wanted to know the best location for a sewage outflow pipe (a pipe that dumps "cleaned" sewage from a treatment plant into the ocean), Curt helped determine where to place the pipe so that currents would carry the outflow to sea for mixing and recycling, rather than toward nearby harbors and beaches. When a tanker spilled its oil into the ocean, Curt helped the cleanup crews determine what direction the oil slick would float and how it would disperse over time.

But in 1990 Curt's career took an interesting turn. His mother showed him an article in a local newspaper that described a landfall of sneakers—hundreds of them—on beaches near Seattle. No one knew where the sneakers were coming from, and Mrs. Ebbesmeyer figured her son, who studied ocean movements for a living, should be able to find out. Not wanting to disappoint his mother, Curt set out to discover the origin of the sneakers. He began his investigation at the beach.

"I just wandered along the coast and asked about the sneakers," he says. "Eventually beachcombers started to call me."

Beachcombers are folks who spend a great deal of time searching for interesting things at the ocean shore. Many beachcombers collect natural objects, like shells, rocks, and seeds. Others collect man-made objects, like jewelry, coins, and anything else that washes ashore or is left behind at the beach. The

beachcombers Curt met told him stories of sneakers washing ashore all along the western coast of North America. Soon Curt had verified reports of beached sneakers as far north as the Queen Charlotte Islands in Canada and as far south as the border of Oregon and California in the United States. Since all the sneakers washing up were the same brand, Curt contacted the company that manufactured them. After many months—and many phone calls—officials in the Nike transportation department gave him the information he was looking for: they had lost five containers full of sneakers off a cargo ship in May. Slowly Curt gathered the details.

The ship, called the *Hansa Carrier*, had been carrying goods from Korea to the United States. It was loaded to capacity when it collided with a vicious storm in the northern Pacific Ocean. Storms on the high seas are serious business, and the one that surprised the *Hansa Carrier* on May 27, 1990, was no exception. Winds whipped at speeds close to sixty miles per hour, churning the sea into waves that were taller than the average two-story home. Weather of this intensity will endanger any ship on the sea, even a six-hundred-foot shipping vessel weighted down with 35,000 tons of cargo. The *Hansa Carrier* managed to pass through the storm intact, but twenty-one of the cargo containers

Curt's mother, Mrs. Genevieve Ebbesmeyer, holds a pair of Nike sneakers found on a West Coast beach during the winter of 1990.

5

A fully loaded cargo container can weigh more than 60,000 pounds. Hundreds of them are routinely stacked on the decks of busy cargo ships.

intact, but twenty-one of the cargo containers on its deck had been tossed into the Pacific Ocean. Five of these containers were packed full of Nike sneakers.

Cargo containers are giant metal boxes that look an awful lot like the back end of a tractor-trailer truck (without the eighteen wheels). They are used to ship manufactured goods across the ocean and can hold any-thing from perfume to toys to sneakers. The inside, or hull, of one cargo ship can hold thousands of containers, and it is not unusual for hundreds more to be stacked on the deck. Although they are tied down with cables, containers stored on the deck can, and do,

fall overboard. In fact, Curt estimates between two thousand and ten thousand containers fall from cargo ships every year. What happens to these containers when they hit the sea? If sealed, the containers can float, creating a dangerous obstacle course for ships and sailors around the world. More often, however, containers are punctured or ripped open during their fall from the ship. These will fill with water and sink to the ocean floor, often releasing their contents into the sea. What happens to the contents themselves? They will float or sink, depend-ing on what they are made of. As Curt learned, sneakers float . . . for a long time.

6

By 1993, three years after the spill, Curt had collected a lot of information about the sneakers. With the help of beachcombers around the world, he had recovered thousands of washed-up Nike running sneakers. Using serial numbers provided by the manufacturer, he could identify which of these were spilled from the *Hansa Carrier*. Most important, he had located the ship's log and now knew exactly where in the Pacific Ocean the *Hansa Carrier* had lost its cargo. Although it started as an interesting hobby undertaken to satisfy his mother's curiosity, the sneaker chase had become much, much more. Curt believed the sneaker spill represented the greatest oceanographic drift experiment of all time. He also believed that the information he had collected told a great deal about the movement of ocean currents in the Pacific Ocean.

A boatload of sneakers from the Hansa Carrier *spill. They were recovered over several years by beachcomber John Anderson of Forks, Washington.*

LONGITUDE AND LATITUDE

Finding a certain place in your town—for example, your friend's house—is fairly straightforward. A city map, a street name, and a house number will lead you right to your friend's door. Finding a certain place in the ocean—for example, the place where the *Hansa Carrier* lost its cargo—is harder. The ocean is not divided into towns and streets and there are few visual landmarks. How, then, do sailors and oceanographers find their way? The answer lies in a planet-wide grid system that has been created to allow a precise definition of any spot on earth. The grid system is made of imaginary lines that run east to west (these are called lines of latitude) and north to south (these are called lines of longitude) around the globe.

Although lines of latitude and longitude are not physical, they are included on most world maps and globes and they represent real positions on the planet. The lines that record latitude are called parallels, because they circle the globe in parallel rings between the North Pole and the South Pole. The lines that record longitude, on the other hand, are not parallel and are called meridians. By choosing one parallel and one meridian as a point of reference, scientists can use this grid system to pinpoint any location on the planet. The reference parallel is the one located exactly midway between the North Pole and the South Pole; you know it as the equator. The reference meridian is the one that passes through the Royal Observatory at Greenwich, England (this location was chosen by international agreement in 1884); we call this line the prime meridian. Every location on the planet can be described by measuring its distance, in degrees (°), from these two reference points. Latitude is measured from the equator (0°) to the North Pole (90°N) or to the South Pole (90°S). Likewise, longitude is measured from the prime meridian (0°) to the meridian located exactly halfway (180°) around the globe. This meridian is called the International Date Line.

The captain of the *Hansa Carrier* recorded his ship's location at the time of the sneaker spill as 48 degrees north latitude and 161 degrees west longitude, or 48°N and 161°W. To find this spot on a map, first find the parallel line located 48 degrees north of the equator. Then find the meridian located 161 degrees west of the prime meridian. The place where these two lines cross is the location of the spill.

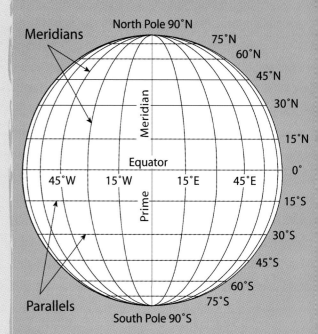

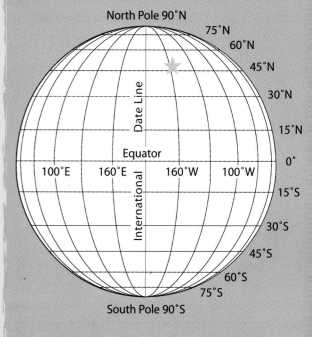

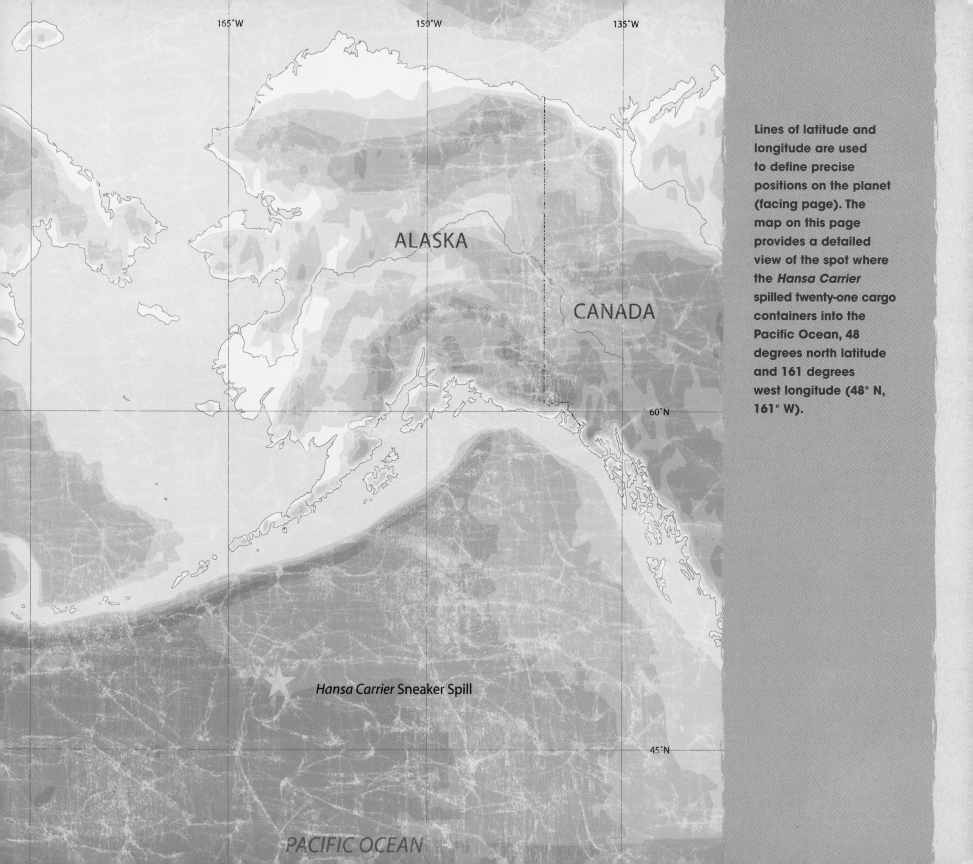

165°W   150°W   135°W

ALASKA

CANADA

60°N

Lines of latitude and longitude are used to define precise positions on the planet (facing page). The map on this page provides a detailed view of the spot where the *Hansa Carrier* spilled twenty-one cargo containers into the Pacific Ocean, 48 degrees north latitude and 161 degrees west longitude (48° N, 161° W).

Hansa Carrier Sneaker Spill

45°N

PACIFIC OCEAN

*Stand for a moment on an ocean
shore almost anywhere in the world
and you will see the ocean move.*

The Science of Ocean Motion

The paper inside this drift bottle instructs the finder to report the bottle's recovery to the scientists who released it.

NOTICE TO FINDER   **NOTICIA A QUIEN ENCUENTRE ESTA TA**

These cards are being used to study the currents of the Pacific Ocean. Please fill spaces. Mail *every* card you find. No postage needed in U.S. In return you will b time and place of their release. Thank you.

Your name   **Su nombre**   Your address   Su

Exact location of card   Date and hour found
Localidad exacta en donde fué hallada la tarjeta   Fecha y hora en que fué hallada la

Si esta tarjeta es enviada de México necesita ponerle timbre de correo. Directa embolsaremos a usted por el importe del mismo. Estas tarjetas forman parte d que se está llevando a cabo sobre las corrientes del Océano Pacífico. Nos har vicio si llena las líneas en blanco con la información deseada. Favor de env tarjetas que encuentre. En cambio de este servicio, recibirá Ud. una tar fecha y el sitio de donde fué despachada la tarjeta que encontró. Anticipamos por su atención.

17835

Throughout this century, oceanographers have used drifting objects to study the movement of the ocean. Early on, these drift experiments were simple. A scientist would drop hundreds of floating objects—for example, sealed glass bottles—into the sea at a given location. Each bottle included a letter inside containing the scientist's name, address, and phone number. The hope was that anyone finding a bottle would read the note inside, contact the scientist, and describe the final location of the bottle. By recording the longitude and latitude at which the bottle was released and the longitude and latitude at which it was found, scientists began the long process of identifying patterns of movement in the world ocean.

Oceanographers recover a sturdy plastic satellite-trackable float from the ocean. Floats like this have replaced the glass bottles once used to study ocean currents.

The main shortfall of these experiments was the low rate of bottle recovery. For every one hundred bottles dropped into the ocean, only one or two were returned to scientists. The other ninety-eight were either destroyed, damaged at sea, frozen into ice floes, or washed ashore in unpopulated locations where they were never found.

Over time oceanographers improved their drift experiments. In the 1970s glass bottles were replaced with plastic drift equipment, or floats. Floats were made in various shapes and sizes, and eventually scientists began adding satellite tracking devices to them. Just as police departments used satellite tracking equipment to follow the path of a stolen car on land, oceanographers used this equipment to follow the path of their floats on the ocean. They no longer had to wait for beachcombers to find and report bottles, and they no longer had to imagine the paths those bottles traveled at sea. If one hundred satellite-trackable floats were dropped into the ocean, scientists could follow the precise movements of all one hundred floats for weeks, months, or years.

Although satellite-tracked drift experiments brought huge advancements in the study of ocean movement, there were limitations to these studies as well. In the 1990s the equipment necessary for satellite tracking was very expensive, which meant scientists often had to limit the size of their experiments. And while scientists were able to track exact ocean movement in real time by following their floating beacons, the tracking equipment had a limited life span. When the batteries ran down, the experiment was over.

Curt Ebbesmeyer thought the *Hansa Carrier* spill represented a new twist in the study of ocean movement. Since Nike sneakers float, the accidental loss of five containers full—an estimated eighty thousand sneakers—represented the largest (and cheapest) ocean drift experiment ever undertaken. His investigations into the cargo spill and the sneaker recovery had produced data on thousands of sneakers. To see if the information he had collected could, indeed, be useful to science, Curt contacted his good friend and fellow oceanographer W. James Ingraham, Jr.

Jim was a scientist at the National Oceanic and Atmospheric Administration (NOAA). Like Curt, he was interested in oceanic movement. In fact, Jim had spent years perfecting a computer program that could calculate surface current movement in the North Pacific Ocean. The program, called the Ocean Surface CURrent Simulator or OSCURS, uses daily weather measurements recorded across the Pacific Ocean for the past century to estimate surface current movement in the northern Pacific. It is one

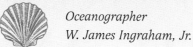
Oceanographer
W. James Ingraham, Jr.

Jim worked as an oceanographer at NOAA's Seattle, Washington, facility for forty-one years.

U.S. DEPARTMENT OF COMMERCE

National Oceanic and Atmospheric Administration

Western Regional Center

7600 Sand Point Way NE

of many computer modeling programs that oceanographers use to fine-tune world surface current maps.

The OSCURS modeling program was of interest to Curt for two reasons. First, OSCURS could answer specific questions about water movement in the North Pacific Ocean. For example, if you input a start date (any day in the past one hundred years) and a specific ocean location (a longitude and latitude), OSCURS could tell you where the water in that location was likely to be on the next day . . . or on the day after that. In fact, OSCURS could tell you where the water was likely to be on any day between the start date and the present day. Second, since objects floating in or on the sea will move with the surface currents, OSCURS represented a powerful means of tracking the floating sneakers.

In 1992, Jim supplied the OSCURS computer program with the sneaker spill data. He input the spill location (North Pacific Ocean at 48 degrees north latitude, 161 degrees west longitude) and the spill date (May 27, 1990) and asked OSCURS to map the drift of the

sneakers over the next year. OSCURS predicted the shoes would land in Vancouver Island on January 31, 1991. In fact, hundreds of sneakers had washed up on Vancouver Island . . . between December 21, 1990, and March 1, 1991. The OSCURS calculations were right on target.

"The OSCURS model is very, very good," says Curt. "Any prediction that is accurate within one month or one hundred miles is pretty darn good. It allows us to reconstruct what happens to a drifting object out there on the ocean."

According to the OSCURS program, sneakers from the Hansa Carrier *spill drifted along the path highlighted with red arrows. Sites of major sneaker recoveries between November 1990 and May 1991 are marked with black circles and the number indicates the amount of sneakers found at each spot.*

"The OSCURS model is very, very good. . . . It allows us to reconstruct what happens to drifting objects out there on the ocean."

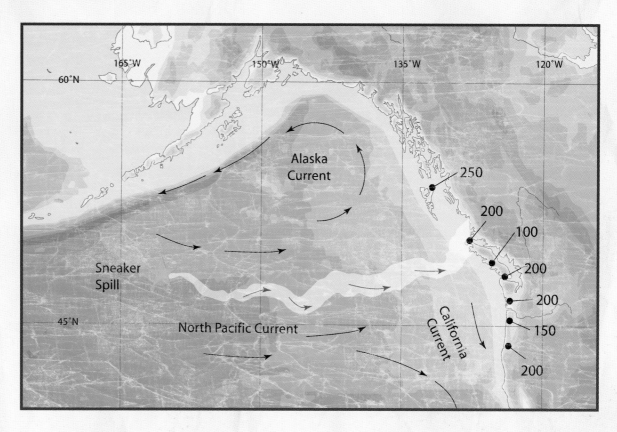

In a hypothetical experiment, OSCURS predicts very different pathways for sneakers dropped at the same location in different calendar years.

The OSCURS reconstruction of the sneaker drift verified the data Curt had collected from beachcombers. After the spill, the sneakers had moved due east . . . toward the western coast of North America. They were most likely carried on the North Pacific Current, a west-to-east traveling surface current flowing in that area. Near the North American coast, the North Pacific Current splits into two separate currents, the north-flowing Alaska Current and the south-flowing California Current. The OSCURS model predicted sneakers washing up along the shores these two currents pass, and beachcombers did indeed find sneakers on these shores.

What about the rest of the sneakers? OSCURS predicted they would continue to float with surface currents around the Pacific Ocean. Once again, beachcombing data verified this prediction: several sneakers from the *Hansa Carrier* spill were found on the northern coast of Hawaii in 1993.

"The sneakers that washed up in Hawaii were quite wearable after three years at sea, and the serial numbers were intact," says Curt. "It is possible they could float for many, many years."

To show the significance of their sneaker-tracking data, Curt and Jim designed an experiment to look more closely at the movement of surface currents in the Pacific Ocean. They asked OSCURS to map the path the spilled sneakers would have followed had they been dropped at the same location in the North Pacific Ocean on May 27 of every year between 1946 and 1990. Because the weather measurement data that OSCURS uses to calculate surface currents has been collected every single day for more than one hundred years, this experiment was easy to do.

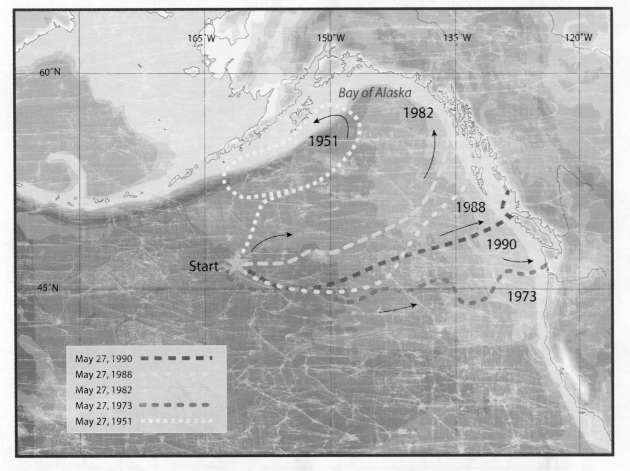

Bay of Alaska

1982

1951

1988

1990

1973

Start

60°N

45°N

165°W 150°W 135°W 120°W

May 27, 1990
May 27, 1988
May 27, 1982
May 27, 1973
May 27, 1951

OSCURS predicted that the drift of the sneakers would have been very different from year to year. Some years the sneakers would have drifted east of the spill site and landed on beaches in Canada (as was the case with the actual spill in 1990). In other years, however, according to the OSCURS prediction, the sneakers would have followed a different path. In 1951, for example, the sneakers would have floated at sea much longer than they did in 1990. That year, OSCURS predicted the sneakers would have traveled in a current-driven circle around the Bay of Alaska.

These results highlight an interesting property of surface currents: variability. Although they flow in the same general location and direction each year, the exact boundaries of the currents shift from season to season and from year to year. Information about these shifts can be useful for marine biologists and other scientists, because it helps them to understand changes in fish populations, patterns of sea life migration, and other ocean events. What causes the slight changes in the position of a current? What are the consequences, if any, of these changes? As is usually the case, good science leads to good answers . . . and many, many more questions.

Curt and Jim had taken advantage of a man-made disaster and from it derived solid

scientific observations. While some scientists considered tracking trash unprofessional, Curt and Jim were convinced of the usefulness of their work and, quite simply, were hooked on the fun of it. They published the results of their sneaker-tracking studies in 1992. They also continued to spread the word about the sneaker spill, hoping for more recoveries.

Serial numbers located on each sneaker helped Curt to identify sneakers, such as this one, that spilled from the Hansa Carrier.

Imagine you are at the beach building a sandcastle. After a long morning of sculpting you put your shovel aside and break for lunch. When you return one hour later, your castle is under water and your shovel is floating fifty feet from shore. You've just witnessed the action of the most visible of ocean movements: waves and tides.

Waves are formed when energy from some external source passes through water. A boat or swimmer can cause waves, as can an underwater explosion, an earthquake, or a gust of wind. On the open ocean, waves can travel huge distances, sometimes moving for hundreds or even thousands of miles before crashing on the beach and leveling your sandcastle. Despite the long distance waves can travel, the water through which they pass moves very little. To prove this, watch your shovel floating offshore. As waves travel toward the beach, they pass under the shovel. With each passing wave, the shovel rises up slightly in the water and then, when the wave has passed by, settles back down. The shovel makes very little progress toward the beach, even though wave after wave passes under it.

Tides, like waves, are easy to see. They are the result of the gravitational pull of the moon—and to a lesser degree the sun—on the ocean. In most places tides result in water-level changes of about six feet. This means that if you were to stand on the beach at high tide so that the ocean was just able to touch your toes, and then waited for low tide (a six-hour wait!), you would have to walk about six feet toward the ocean in order to have your toes touch the water again. It also means that if you leave a sandcastle within six feet of the low tide, you are likely to find it demolished when you return at high tide.

Unlike waves and tides, ocean currents are much harder to see. They are driven by complicated forces that include wind systems, the rotation of the planet, and variations in water temperature, density, and saltiness. The sum total of these forces is strong currents that move in fairly predictable patterns.

The currents that move water from the sea surface down to the sea floor, across the sea floor, and from the sea floor back up to the surface are known as deep sea currents. Since waters from the deep ocean are rich in the nutrients required to feed the animals and plants that live at the ocean's surface, deep sea currents are crucial to the maintenance of a vigorous and healthy sea. They ensure that these nutrients are continuously cycled from the bottom of the ocean back up to its surface.

Surface currents, which move water in the uppermost part of the sea, are the currents most important to the tracking of flotsam and jetsam. Just as your breath blown across the surface of a bowl of water would push the water in a particular path, the wind systems that blow across the world ocean, in combination with the forces listed above, create a predictable pattern of surface currents. As you can see on the map on the next page, the surface currents in many locations combine to create large circular patterns of ocean movement. These swirls of current are called gyres (pronounced jīrz). Although smaller ones do exist, the five major gyres are found in the North Pacific Ocean, the South Pacific Ocean, the North Atlantic Ocean, the South Atlantic Ocean, and the Indian Ocean.

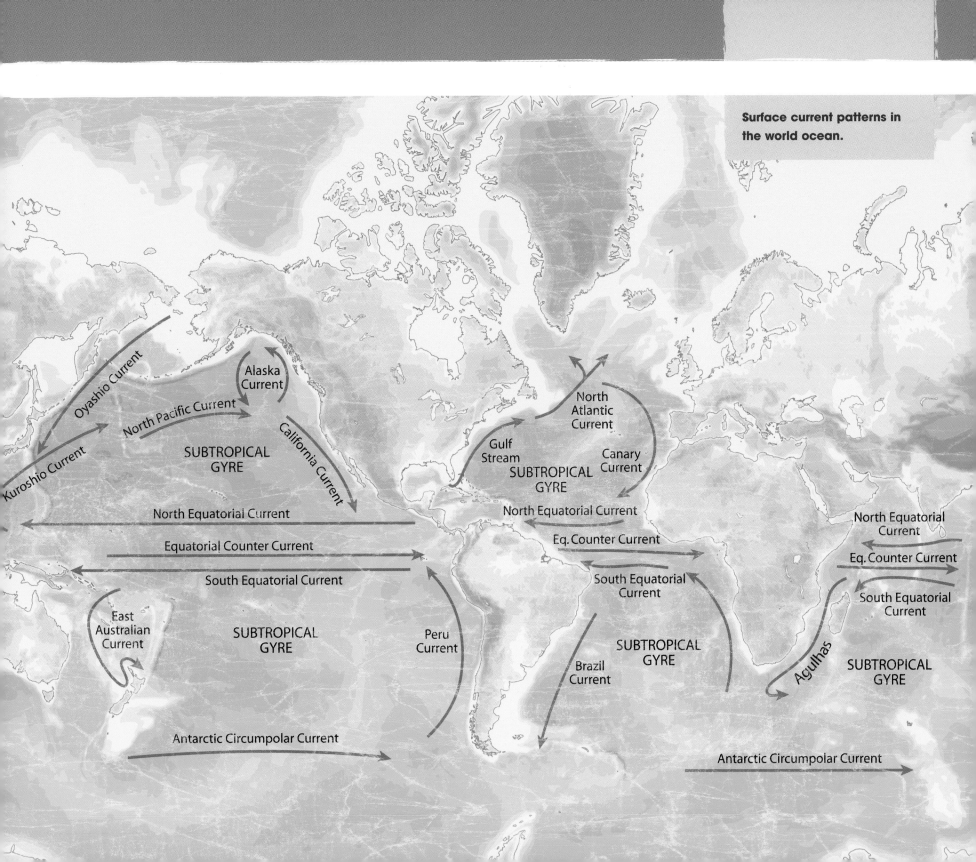

Surface current patterns in the world ocean.

CHAPTER THREE

Another Day, Another Spill

While they waited for more sneakers from the *Hansa Carrier* spill to wash ashore, Curt Ebbesmeyer and Jim Ingraham heard about another cargo spill that they could use to learn about ocean currents. The details were similar to those of the sneaker spill. A cargo ship en route from Asia to North America hit a storm in the North Pacific Ocean and lost twelve containers overboard. One of those containers held 28,800 floating bathtub toys: yellow ducks, blue turtles, red beavers, and green frogs. The tub toys were originally packaged in sets of four (one of each animal), but beachcombers found hundreds of individual toys along Alaskan beaches, suggesting that the plastic and cardboard packaging had dissolved at sea. To Curt and Jim, this meant that thousands of the most floatable of all floatable objects were adrift on the ocean.

Plastic tub toys like the ones lost in the 1992 cargo spill.

As with the sneaker spill, Curt had to track down the important details of the tub toy spill himself. He managed to find out the exact location of the spill, the specific contents of the container, and even the length of time it took for the cardboard and plastic packaging to disintegrate and release the tub toys into the ocean. (This last bit of information, by the way, was acquired with a simple experiment conducted in Curt's yard. He filled a large bucket with seawater and dropped in unopened packages of tub toys bought at local stores. In less than twenty-four hours, the cardboard packaging had deteriorated enough to release the package contents.) Curt also placed advertisements in newspapers encouraging beachcombers to report any tub toys they found.

Meanwhile, Jim set to work feeding the new spill data to OSCURS. He input the start location (45 degrees north latitude and 178 degrees east longitude) and the start date (January 10, 1992) and asked OSCURS to map the drift of the tub toys over the next year. OSCURS predicted that the toys would begin washing ashore in May 1993. In fact, the first tub toys had washed ashore in Alaska six months earlier than that, on November 16, 1992. Despite what you might think, Jim wasn't worried about this discrepancy. In fact, he had anticipated it. He had seen many a

floating sneaker during the previous years, and he knew how they floated: low in the water with most of the shoe submerged. Tub toys, on the other hand, float with almost their entire surface above the water. On the open ocean, both objects will drift with the surface currents. But the tub toys will also be pushed along by winds and, as a result, can travel much faster than the current. Scientists call this property windage.

"We knew the tub toys would travel faster than the currents," says Jim. "But we didn't know how much faster."

Once he had determined the windage for the tub toys, Jim was able to adjust the OSCURS program so that it accounted for this factor in all its simulations of tub toy movement. With this adjustment in place, OSCURS predicted the correct landing location (Alaska) and time (November 1992) for the tub toys.

As this tank test demonstrates, a sneaker and a rubber duck float very differently.

23

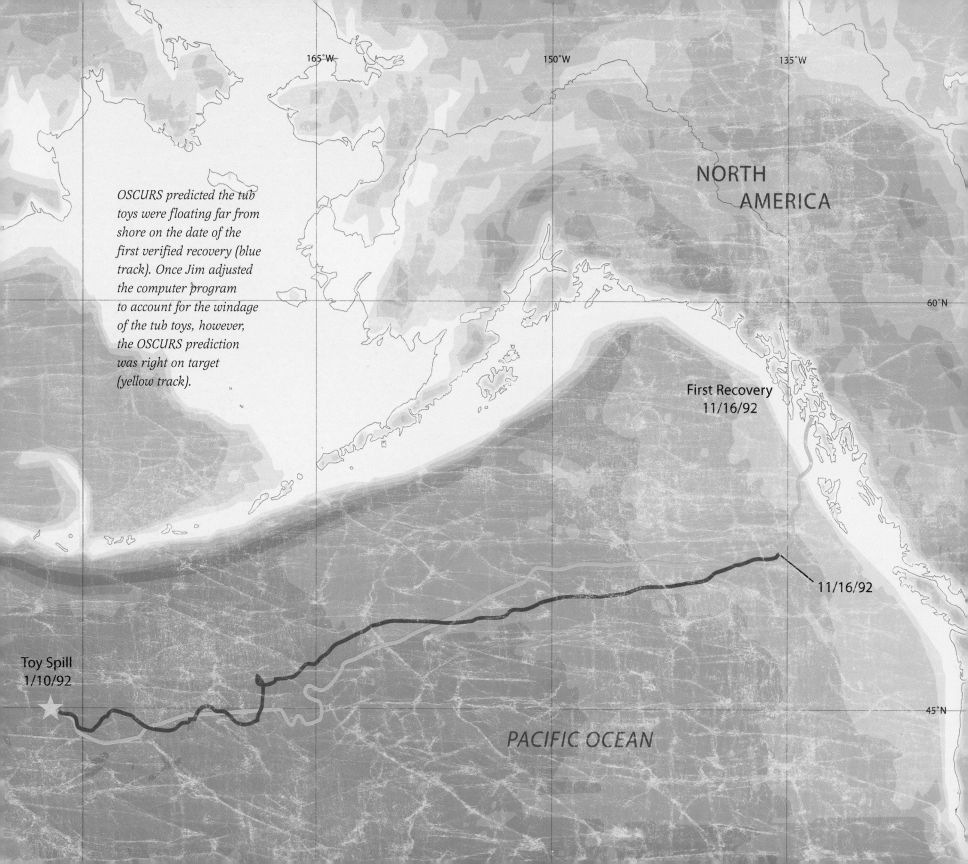

165°W

150°W

135°W

NORTH
AMERICA

60°N

*OSCURS predicted the tub
toys were floating far from
shore on the date of the
first verified recovery (blue
track). Once Jim adjusted
the computer program
to account for the windage
of the tub toys, however,
the OSCURS prediction
was right on target
(yellow track).*

First Recovery
11/16/92

11/16/92

Toy Spill
1/10/92

45°N

PACIFIC OCEAN

As they had done with the sneaker spill, Curt and Jim performed an experiment in which they asked OSCURS to map the route the tub toys would have drifted had they spilled on January 10 of every year between 1946 and 1993. Once again, the drift paths changed dramatically from year to year. The drift path for 1992, the actual year of the spill, traveled farthest north and led Curt to predict that the tub toy spill would fuel ocean current research for years to come. In a 1992 publication of their data he said, "After a number of years we expect some of the toys to be dispersed around the North Pacific Ocean, the Arctic Ocean, and the northern Atlantic Ocean. Given the substantial release of 29,000 toy animals, we anticipate that by the year 2000 a few toys will have been transported to many oceanic locations in the Northern Hemisphere."

To help track the tub toys over the next decade, and to prepare for future spills, Curt and Jim founded the Beachcombers' and Oceanographers' International Association,

The first issue of the Beachcombers' Alert! *newsletter was published in 1996. Since then Curt and his colleagues at the Beachcombers' and Oceanographers' International Association have published four editions a year.*

Beachcombers' Alert! ™

Since 1996

VOL. 9 No. 2 • OCTOBER - DECEMBER 2004 • CURTIS C. EBBESMEYER, Ph.D.

Beachcombing Science

Dean Orbison with turtles, ducks, beavers, and frogs.
After 12 years adrift, the frogs and turtles remained true-blue to their original colors (green and blue, respectively), whereas the ducks and beavers faded from yellow and red to white, respectively. Dorothy Orbison photo

Beachcombing Science From Bathtub Toys
by Curtis C. Ebbesmeyer

Twelve years and counting — the saga of the tots' tub toys continues. On January 10, 1992, 28,800 turtles, ducks, beavers and frogs packed in a cargo container — called *Floatees* by the manufacturer — splashed into the mid-Pacific, where the 45th parallel intersects the International Date Line (44.7°N, 178.1°E). During August-September, 1992, after 2,200 miles adrift, hundreds

Continued on page 2

The Call of Our Dust

46,000 by Richard Lang and Judith Selby. After years adrift, the bathtub toys (left) disintegrate to bits of floating plastic. "The California Coastal Commission reports 46,000 pieces of visible plastic floating in every square mile of the ocean. This shocking fact along with our inability to visualize the magnitude of that quantity compelled us to count and attempt to exhibit 46,000 plastic pieces collected from Northern California beaches," wrote the artists. "When we committed to this work, we had no idea of the enormity of the undertaking. To date, we continue our task. On a hundred wires, we strung 4,600 pieces of plastic to simulate the colorful bits of plastic floating in 1/10 of a square mile of sea."

Multiplying 46,000 plastic pieces per square mile by the total area of the ocean yields 6.4 trillion pieces of visible plastic afloat on earth, equivalent to a thousand pieces per earthling. The U.S. Environmental Protection Agency estimates that Americans annually make 910 million trips to the beach. If the ocean transported all these bits to U.S. shores, Americans could rid the sea of visible plastic by picking up seven thousand bits per trip. Copyright photo by Richard Lang and Judith Selby.

Continued on page 4

Beachcombers Dean and Tyler Orbison found this yellow duck, as well as 110 other tub toys, on remote beaches in Alaska.

a nonprofit organization dedicated to keeping beachcombers aware of commercial flotsam circulating in the world's oceans. The association has published its newsletter, *Beachcombers' Alert!*, since 1996. Curt and Jim also began attending beachcomber fairs, festivals at which beachcombers gather to show their finds and discuss issues important to oceans and beaches. These events quickly became a crucial part of Curt's unique brand of oceanography.

"It is at the fairs that we pick up hints of ongoing container spills," Curt says. "And when we attend these fairs much happens by serendipity."

It was at a fair in Sitka, Alaska, for example, that Curt met Dean Orbison and his son Tyler. The father-and-son team had been beachcombing together for years by the time they hauled their basket of 111 bathtub toys into the 2004 Sitka fair. Curt was elated.

"Dean and Tyler beachcombed an important contribution to oceanographic science; they patiently recorded the recovery dates and locations for ninety of the toys over the course of twelve years."

To Curt, this information was an oceanographic gold mine. He quickly noticed a pattern underlying the Orbisons' recovery data: every two or three years, they found an unusually large number of tub toys. In the intervening years, on the other hand, many fewer toys washed ashore. Since the Orbison beachcombing logs showed that the pair had spent a consistent amount of time scouring beaches each season, Curt suspected that the toy-recovery pattern had something to do with the path the toys were following in the ocean. He theorized that the toys were circling around the Gulf of Alaska, as OSCURS simulations had suggested they would, and that each circle was taking two years.

"The Orbison data indicate flotsam wheeling around the North Pacific Subpolar Gyre for up to four circuits," he says. "The first circuit was faster than the latter three, perhaps because the toys developed holes but continued floating."

With his typical flair, Curt tested this idea by drilling holes into a rubber duck and throwing it into his test tank: a bucket of seawater. The hole-y ducks did indeed float. But they did not float as upright as the unaltered ducks did, and they filled with water. Curt believes the damaged and waterlogged tub toys drift more slowly over time.

Fifteen years after the spill, Curt continues to receive telephone calls, letters, and e-mails every month reporting rubber tub toys found on beaches around the world. Many of these reports don't hold up to close scrutiny (you would be surprised how many *other* rubber ducks get lost at the beach). But occasionally toys from the 1992 spill are recovered. In 2003 two exciting reports were received: a duck was found on the eastern coast of the United States and a frog was

Curt confers with beachcombers at a Washington fair (top) and on an Alaskan beach (bottom).

Every month Curt receives phone calls, letters, and e-mails reporting rubber tub toys found on beaches around the world.

recovered in Scotland. Both reports suggest that OSCURS trajectories were accurate and that some of the tub toys had managed to move into the Bering Sea and complete a treacherous journey across the Arctic Ocean.

Between his newsletter and the beachcomber fairs, Curt stays in close contact with the beachcombing community. If there is a cargo spill, he hears about it. And it seems there are always new spills. On December 9, 1994, the *Hyundai Seattle* dropped a container holding 34,000 hockey gloves. The gloves floated. On February 20, 1996, the *Ocean Orchid* lost 1,100 fir logs in the center of the Gulf of Alaska. The two-hundred-foot-long logs floated. On February 13, 1997, containers lost from the *Tokio Express* dumped 4,756,940 plastic LEGO pieces into the Atlantic Ocean. The colorful plastic pieces floated. And in December 2002, another 33,000 sneakers fell into the Pacific Ocean. The list of floating trash goes on and on, and Curt and Jim continue to track it.

Debris Curt Is Currently Tracking

ITEM	SPILL DATE	SPILL LOCATION
Nike sneakers	May 27, 1990	Pacific Ocean
Bathtub toys	January 10, 1992	Pacific Ocean
Hockey gloves	December 9, 1994	Pacific Ocean
Fir logs	February 20, 1996	Bay of Alaska
LEGO pieces	February 13, 1997	Atlantic Ocean
Nike sneakers	December 1999	Pacific Ocean
Computer monitors, etc.	January 2000	Pacific Ocean
Plastic soap dispensers	March 2001	Pacific Ocean
Nike sneakers, etc.	December 2002	Pacific Ocean

S neakers, tub toys, and marine debris are not the only things carried by surface currents. In fact, an entire class of marine creatures relies on surface currents to move them around the ocean. Scientists call these creatures plankton (a name derived from the Greek word for "wandering," *planktos*), and they can be grouped in many different ways. One kind of plankton, called holoplankton, spend their entire lives drifting on currents, while another group, known as meroplankton, spend only the earliest part of their lives this way. Phytoplankton use the energy of sunlight to make their own food, whereas zooplankton eat smaller organisms to survive. Macroplankton are large and microplankton are so small that powerful microscopes are needed in order to see them. No matter which of the categories they

Tiny planktonic organisms known as diatoms (top) and copepods (bottom, among strands of algae) are best viewed through a microscope.

Floating seaweed, such as this kelp, drifts with surface currents and provides shelter and protection for various marine organisms.

Purple striped jellyfish (facing page, left) and walleye pollock (facing page, right) are two creatures that live at least part of their lives as plankton.

30

fall into, all plankton—from microscopic diatoms and copepods to larger kelps and jellyfish—depend on ocean currents for their survival.

Consider, for example, the walleye pollock. Female fish of this species release millions of eggs during a short period each spring. Once fertilized, the pollock larvae drift in the ocean currents for two weeks until hatching. Once hatched, the baby pollock continue to exist as plankton, floating at the mercy of the currents until they develop the ability to swim. (Walleye pollock would be classified, by the way, as meroplankton, zooplankton, and macroplankton!) During their planktonic existence, baby walleye pollock are extremely susceptible to predators, including their own parents. Studies have shown that pollock adults will freely eat pollock babies if given the chance. This got the scientists who study these fish wondering: could the good pollock years (years in which fishermen catch lots and lots of pollock) be a result of good currents? That is, do more baby pollocks survive to adulthood in these years because the currents carry them farther away from where hungry adult pollock live? If this was true, then bad pollock years would correlate with years in which current movement did not carry the planktonic walleye pollock babies far enough from their parents.

Since female pollock spawn in the same ocean location at approximately the same time each year, scientists were able to use OSCURS to simulate the movement of the currents in the spawning area every year for the past one hundred years. By comparing the currents simulated by OSCURS with the number of walleye pollock caught in each year, these scientists were able to gather evidence to support their theory. One of the factors that affect yearly walleye pollock population *is* surface currents in their spawning area. This is just one small example of how ocean currents can have an impact on the distribution of fish in the sea . . . and figuring out the distribution of fish in the sea is just one more reason that understanding ocean currents is important to all of us.

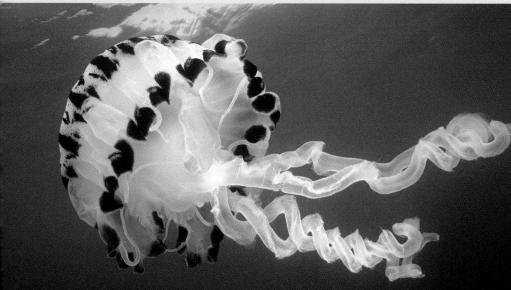

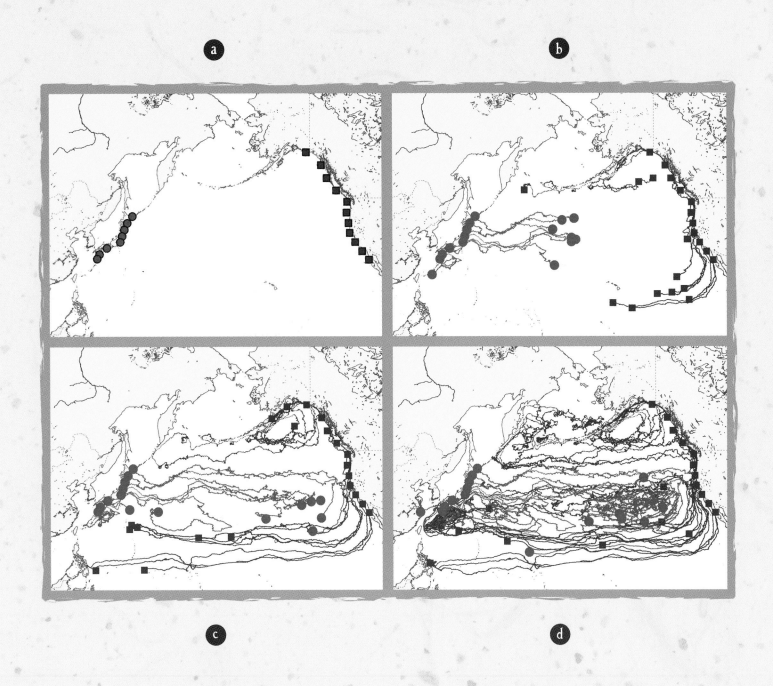

CHAPTER FOUR

The Garbage Patch

What would happen if you released a floating object (any floating object will do) from a handful of different locations along the Pacific coasts of Asia and North America and then followed those objects as they drifted around the ocean for thirty years? An experiment of this nature would, of course, be almost impossible to carry out in real life. But it can be carried out fairly easily by a computer program like OSCURS. Jim Ingraham designed just such an experiment, and after one full week of constant computing, OSCURS provided details on what the long-term movement of these drifting objects might look like.

In this hypothetical experiment, OSCURS simulated the movement of drifting objects released from locations along the Pacific coast of North America and Asia (a). After six months (b) and three years (c) afloat, the drifters are moving in a manner consistent with the currents that make up the North Pacific Subtropical Gyre. After ten years afloat (d), the drifters have begun to collect in two specific areas of the gyre.

At the beginning of the experiment, the hypothetical drifters seemed to move just as one might expect: in a large loop around the North Pacific Gyre. In the later stages of the experiment, however, the pattern changed. After ten years, for example, many of the hypothetical objects seemed to collect in a small portion of the gyre. After twenty years afloat, the drifters continued to collect in this area, and in a second area located on the opposite edge of the gyre. After thirty years afloat, a great many of the hypothetical drifters had become trapped in the two small areas on the edges of the gyre.

At about the same time Jim was running experiments of this sort with OSCURS, Captain Charles Moore was sailing his ocean research vessel *Alguita* through the North Pacific Subtropical Gyre. Partway between Hawaii and California, Charlie and his crew found a floating patch of garbage unlike any they had ever seen.

"There were shampoo caps and soap bottles and plastic bags and fishing floats as far as I could see. Here I was in the middle of the ocean, and there was nowhere I could go to avoid the plastic," Charlie remembers. "It seemed unbelievable, but I never found a clear spot. In the week it took to cross, no matter what time of day I looked, plastic debris was floating everywhere."

Charlie had discovered the Eastern Garbage Patch. Its location coincided exactly with the place Jim's hypothetical drifters collected in the OSCURS long-term drift experiment. As it turns out, the Garbage Patch lies in a convergence zone, an area of the ocean where numerous currents come together and force surface waters to sink. This sinking of surface waters is called down-welling, and it feeds the network of currents that flow in the deep sea. Floating debris follows the surface waters into the convergence zone but cannot follow it downward as it sinks; instead, the trash accumulates at the sea surface. So debris is continually brought into the convergence zone, but it cannot easily leave it. The result is a floating garbage dump that is as big as the state of Alaska.

Charlie estimated that the *Alguita* had passed through three million tons of trash as it crossed the Garbage Patch, and he arrived home determined to test that number. As founder of the Algalita Marine Research Foundation (AMRF), a nonprofit organization devoted to preservation of the marine environment, he was in a good position to do so. With the help of Curt, Jim, and other colleagues, Charlie designed an ambitious experiment to calculate exactly how much plastic—and, for comparison, how much zooplankton—was floating in the Garbage Patch. In 1998, he and his crew

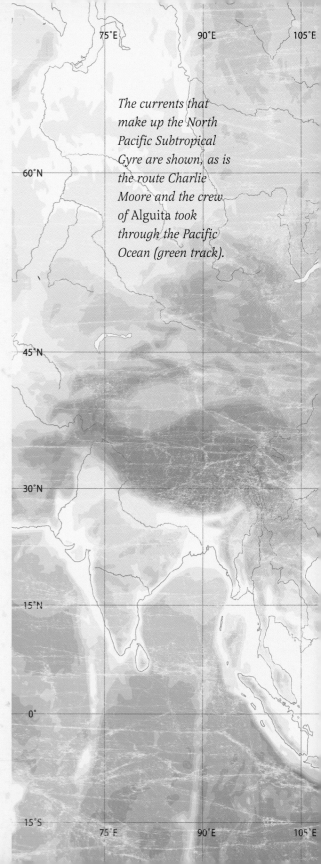

The currents that make up the North Pacific Subtropical Gyre are shown, as is the route Charlie Moore and the crew of Alguita *took through the Pacific Ocean (green track).*

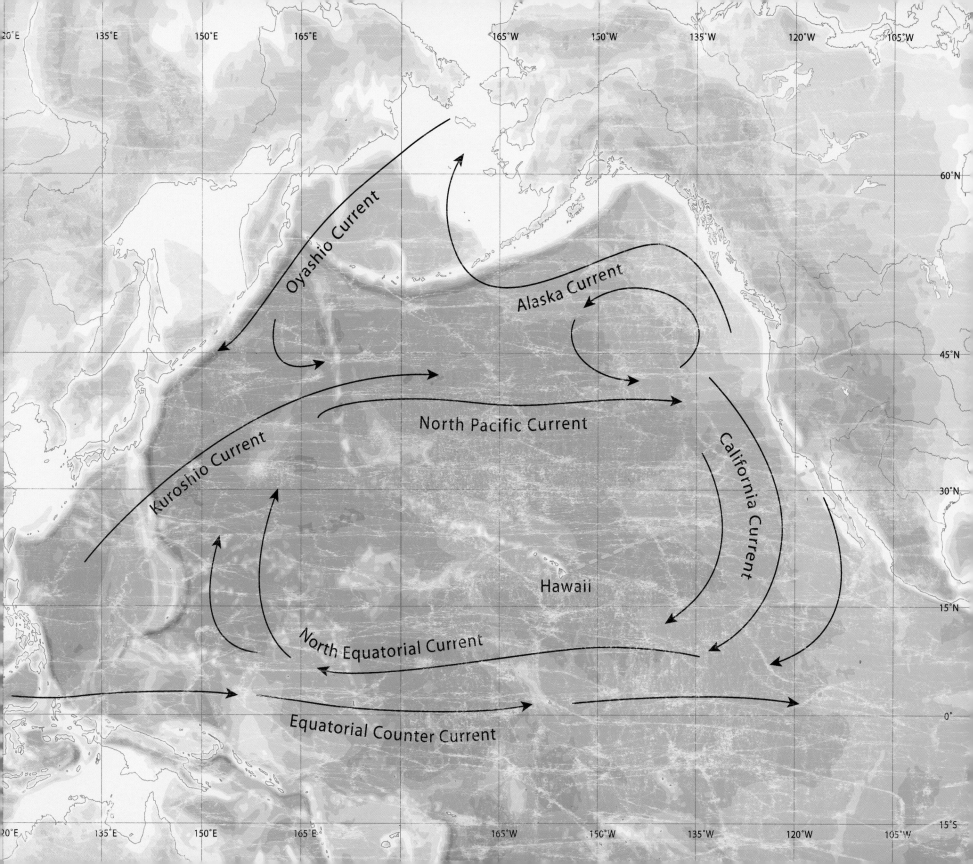

A manta trawl is used to collect objects floating at the surface of the ocean.

net. Anything smaller than the holes in the net will flow through; anything larger will be captured. At the end of the experiment, the material caught in the net is collected for analysis. Charlie and his crew used a manta trawl to collect samples from different locations in the Garbage Patch.

Back in the laboratory, AMRF scientists used a microscope and a pair of tweezers to separate each and every piece of plastic in these samples, as well as each and every particle of zooplankton. These samples were then dried thoroughly and weighed. The results from this experiment were grim: for every pound of zooplankton that Charlie and his crew found in the Garbage Patch, they found six pounds of plastic.

Charlie and his research team have returned to the gyre several times, and each time they have found similar plastic contamination. In 2005 they used a new type of trawl that would allow them to analyze the amount of plastic below the surface of the sea.

"The point of that study," says Charlie, "was to prove the aptness of the biblical adage 'seek and ye shall find.' There is plastic at the surface of the ocean and there is plastic below the surface, too. In fact, we have not found any place free from plastic pollution."

Where is all of this plastic coming from? Some of it, of course, falls off cargo ships or fishing vessels: floating sneakers, plastic tub

returned to the Eastern Garbage Patch with a manta trawl.

A manta trawl is a collection net that can be pulled behind a research vessel. It consists of a long net attached to a winged metal box. The wings keep the box afloat so that water at the surface of the ocean can be forced through it and into the net. All the objects floating on the surface of the sea are also forced through the metal box and into the

toys, abandoned fishing nets, and similar items can all be found in the Garbage Patch. But Charlie estimates that these sources account for only 20 percent of the plastic debris on the ocean. The other 80 percent, he says, arrives in the ocean by way of land-based rivers and storm drains. The water reaching the ocean from these sources is often full of plastic, including everything from litter (discarded beverage bottles, plastic containers of all shapes and sizes, lost toys — the list is endless) to manufacturing waste (tiny plastic bits, called nurdles, that manufacturers produce as a precursor to larger plastic items). Almost all of this plastic trash floats, and much of it collects in the Garbage Patch.

What happens to this plastic trash during the decades it floats around the Garbage Patch? Not much, because plastic is one of the most indestructible materials on the planet. This is one of the reasons we find it so useful. Plastic is found in everything, from the toys we play with to the plates we eat from, the cars we drive, and even the clothes we wear.

Charlie Moore holds a plastic-filled seawater sample pulled from the area of the Pacific Ocean known as the Eastern Garbage Patch.

Unfortunately, the very property that makes plastic a useful material for all these items makes it virtually impossible to get rid of. There is no organism anywhere on the planet that can digest plastic. A long exposure to sunshine, wind, and waves will eventually break plastic objects into smaller and smaller pieces of plastic, but those small pieces are still made entirely of indestructible, undigestable plastic.

As if that weren't bad enough, studies have shown that plastic particles, even the tiniest pieces, interact with contaminants in the ocean. Like microscopic sponges, the plastic bits soak up oily pollutants as they float in the sea. Sea turtles are known to mistake small, round plastic bits for fish eggs, and larger creatures, like salps and jellyfish, filter the particles out of the water. These bits of plastic and the contaminants they carry can end up in our own food chain when those jellyfish are eaten by fish

 This plastic-filled northern fulmar carcass (bottom) was found on a beach in Washington. The fifty-nine plastic pieces found inside it (above) weighed more than sixteen grams, or just over half an ounce.

that are, in turn, caught by commercial fisherman.

Even larger pieces of plastic debris have been shown to wreak havoc on marine creatures. Bottle caps and disposable lighters are seen in the carcasses of sea birds found on beaches from Hawaii to Washington. Apparently the birds are mistaking floating plastic for food. Many of these birds die of starvation because the plastic filling their stomachs can be neither digested nor excreted. Discarded fishing nets and other fishing gear can tangle and drown fish, sea turtles, seals, and other animals. Experts now estimate that the number of marine mammals in the Pacific Ocean that die each year due to plastic ingestion and net entanglement approaches 100,000.

Plastic that does not get trapped in the Garbage Patch or eaten by a marine creature can, eventually, return to shore. Beaches around the world, even those on remote and uninhabited islands, bear the unmistakable marks of a plastic-dependent society. On Kure Atoll, a ring-shaped coral island at the farthest reaches of the Hawaiian island chain, researchers routinely observe a startling array of plastic debris: bottles, buoys, fishing nets, hard hats, soccer balls, sneakers, and tub toys. On the Hawaiian island called Tern, where researchers have collected and stored beached debris for ten years, the despoilment is overwhelming.

 This litter-strewn beach is on Kure Atoll, a remote, uninhabited island in the Pacific Ocean.

"If you turned off the plastic switch somehow," Curt said during a visit to Tern Island in 1999, "you would still have plastic washing ashore here for thirty or forty years. That's how much plastic is out there. I think in our family of creatures we are misbehaving badly."

Charlie Moore agrees. "We humans have got to change the way we produce and consume plastics. And then we have got to hope the ocean can clean itself up in hundreds of years."

Charlie and his colleagues at the Algalita Marine Research Foundation plan to continue tracking trash in the Eastern Garbage Patch and other places in the world ocean. Plans are under way to study plastic debris on the western edge of the North Pacific Gyre as well as in the Indian Ocean Gyre. The results of these studies will help scientists, plastics manufacturers, and policymakers to better understand the extent of plastic pollution in the world ocean and, hopefully, help inspire creative solutions to the problem.

People often ask Curt Ebbesmeyer if we could clean up the plastic in the Eastern Garbage Patch piece by piece. His answer is a firm no.

"It's not practical to clean it up that way," he points out. "It would be like mowing the state of Texas . . . twice."

What we need to do, Curt says, is find a way to stop the plastic before it gets into the ocean. We need to stop using disposable plastics and at the same time invent new biodegradable materials to meet our plastic needs. And while we encourage and wait for these developments to happen, we need to record what we see on the beach.

"We can save the ocean through numbers," says Curt. "We need sentinels on every mile. Walk one mile of beach every day and record what you see. You will be helping the ocean survive."

Just how does this sort of observation help the ocean to survive? Curt believes that the information it provides will make citizens and governments more aware of the plastic pollution problem. And when citizens and governments become more aware of a problem, solutions can be found. There are many environmental organizations that practice what Curt preaches; information on a few of them can be found at the end of this book.

And what if you don't happen to live near a beach? What can you do to help save the oceans?

"Remember the three R's," says Charlie Moore. "Reduce. Reuse. Recycle. The first R has been pretty much neglected. It is not happening enough.

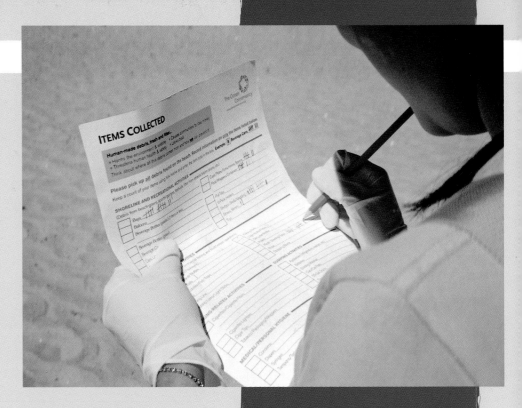

Reduce your use of single-use throwaway plastics. Reduce your use of plastics as much as possible. And tell your friends to do the same thing!"

By monitoring the amount and type of debris collected, participants in coastal cleanup events help the ocean survive.

reduce

recycle

reuse

In Hawaii, scientists and
ecologists from federal, state,
and local agencies have
joined forces to remove net
debris from the ocean . . .
mostly by hand.

CHAPTER FIVE

Monster Debris

In 1991, the same year Curt Ebbesmeyer began hunting for sneakers, scientists in Hawaii found a four-thousand-pound monster in the sea.

"Driving up to it in a small boat, it looked very much like a barely emergent sand islet or reef," remembers Dr. Mary Donohue, one of the team of scientists who eventually captured the beast. "It was so buoyant that we could easily stand on it in the water."

The monster was actually a giant mass of discarded fishing nets that had become hopelessly tangled together at sea. The huge ball of plastic was longer than a school bus and half as heavy.

Ghost nets can tangle marine creatures, such as the sea turtle (top) and Hawaiian monk seal (bottom). Scientists were able to free this tangled turtle, but not the monk seal.

Unfortunately, abandoned nets like this are fairly common. The nets are lost, ripped, or thrown from fishing vessels, and these days they can be found drifting almost anywhere in the world ocean. Scientists call them "ghost nets" because of their eerie ability to continue the work they were designed for—that is, to catch fish—even when they are no longer attached to a fishing boat. As they drift with the currents, ghost nets silently devour everything in their path: fish, turtles, sharks, whales, seals, sea birds, and even trash.

"When an animal gets tangled," explains Mary, "it attracts other predators who feed on the remains and end up entangled themselves."

As if drowning animals weren't bad enough, drifting ghost nets also crush and scrape coral reefs, ruining hundreds of years' worth of coral growth in the crash of a single wave. Mary has seen some of this damage firsthand.

"In some places it looks as if a bulldozer has been driven over the coral reef," she says. "These ghost nets are really destructive."

With the help of dozens of divers, a Coast Guard cutter, and a crane, scientists were eventually able to pull the monstrous ghost net out of the ocean. But surveys conducted by Mary and others found tons—more than fourteen tons, to be exact—

of other ghost nets and net pieces littering the Hawaiian Islands environment. To protect the environment as well as the marine animals that live in it, Mary and her colleagues began a program to find, count, and remove ghost nets. Between 1999 and 2005, this group of dedicated scientists, divers, and ecologists removed five hundred tons of net debris from the area, mostly by hand. Even with this success, however, Mary is realistic about humankind's status in the battle against ghost nets.

"The bottom line," she says, "is that we're making a difference . . . but right now we're barely holding steady."

Three thousand miles away, Colorado researcher Jim Churnside is working to tip the scales in favor of net removal. Like Mary, Jim is studying the ghost net problem, but from an entirely different angle. With the help of Alaskan pilot Tim Veenstra, he is studying ghost nets from the sky. Tim and Jim believe that one way to protect Hawaii's delicate habitat is to remove ghost nets from the Pacific Ocean long before they drift near the islands. But how do you find ghost nets the size of a school bus (and most are much smaller than this) in an ocean that is larger than all seven continents combined? The job would be like trying to find a needle in a haystack . . . unless you know something

"In some places it looks as if a bulldozer has been driven over the coral reef. These ghost nets are really destructive."

Net pieces and other debris, including a plastic laundry basket, blanket fragile coral in Hawaii.

45

The aircraft used to search the Pacific Ocean for ghost nets is also used in hurricane research.

about Pacific Ocean currents and how floating objects drift in them.

"Our first step was to talk to Jim Ingraham about where in the North Pacific Ocean we should look for the ghost nets," says Jim Churnside. "Then we followed his directions to more specific locations using satellites and aircraft."

In 2003, Churnside and Veenstra launched the GhostNet Project. In collaboration with scientists across the country, the two flew over the Garbage Patch using satellite information, radar, and other technologies to spot ghost nets. In three days' time they saw more than one hundred drifting ghost nets . . . and thousands of other types of floating debris.

"There is a lot more trash out there than I expected," says Jim Churnside.

The GhostNet Project continues to monitor the Garbage Patch. The hope is that scientists will eventually be able to use information from satellite pictures of the ocean to determine exactly where ghost nets are. Remember that the exact locations of surface currents can change from year to year. As a result, the exact location of the Garbage Patch changes, too. Combining information from satellites with information from computer models like OSCURS will help scientists to locate the Garbage Patch, and therefore ghost nets, more accurately.

While pilot Tim Veenstra looks out over the Pacific Ocean, scientist Jim Churnside mans the onboard computer. Both are searching for ghost nets.

Charlie Moore and his crew tagged this small ghost net in the Pacific Ocean during their 2005 voyage. The round device in the foreground is the tag.

In the summer of 2005, Churnside and Veenstra started another project, the GhostNet Volunteer Ship Program. They asked ship captains who would be sailing in the Pacific Ocean to carry ghost net tags on their ships. The tags are actually floating buoys equipped with satellite tracking equipment. When captain and crew encounter a ghost net that they are unable to remove from the ocean, they can attach a tag to it. Once a net is tagged, GhostNet scientists can track its movement. If the net drifts near a delicate habitat, like the coral reefs of Hawaii, a ship can be deployed to intercept it before it does any damage.

The first participant in the GhostNet Volunteer Ship Program was none other than Captain Charles Moore. Charlie and the crew of the *Alguita* planned to spend three weeks collecting water samples in the North Pacific Gyre during the summer of 2005. By carrying GhostNet buoys, Charlie and his crew were able to tag ghost nets that they couldn't collect during the voyage. During the three-week trip, they deployed four buoys.

The future of GhostNet cleanup efforts are shown in this drawing. A tagged ghost net is floating in the foreground and the vessel is removing a ghost net. The scene also depicts a UAV (unmanned aerial vehicle) identifying ghost nets from the air and a satellite aiding tracking and communication.

Upon his return, GhostNet scientists sent this message to Charlie:

A fine job indeed, sir! The Ghostnet Program is indebted to the Master and Crew of the ORV *Alguita*. You have deployed the first wave of drifters designed to help us understand how this rubbish moves around the ocean. We are monitoring their paths, and will continue to keep you updated with respect to both their positions and the conclusions we draw concerning the influence of environmental conditions on those movements.

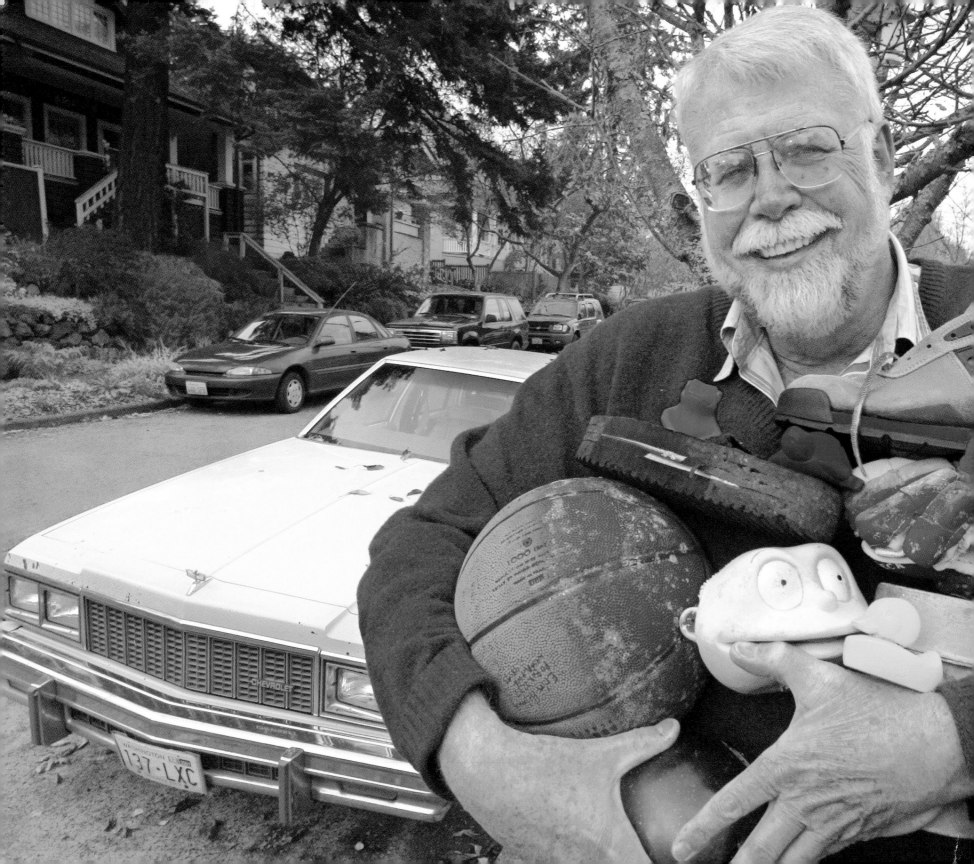

Although tracking ghost nets with satellite equipment is much fancier than tracking sneakers with a network of beachcombers, the end result is the same. The information Curt Ebbesmeyer collects, like the information GhostNet scientists collect, will improve our understanding of how the ocean moves. In the long run, both will help us to protect the ocean and the creatures that live in it.

Now retired from his job as an oceanographic consultant, Curt still spends fifty hours or more each week tracking trash. He continues to publish his newsletter, collect stories from beachcombers around the world, and visit schools to introduce children to the wonders of oceanography. With the help of scientists like Jim Ingraham and Charlie Moore, Curt has awoken the world to the troubling quantity of trash adrift on the oceans. And with the help of scientists like Mary Donohue, Jim Churnside, and Tim Veenstra, he is helping to protect the ocean from the damage this drifting garbage can cause. Even with these accomplishments, however, Curt's motivation for tracking trash remains simple.

"I just like studying the ocean," he says, "and I like to do it in ways that I enjoy." Thinking back to how he got his start in this unusual career, he adds, "And you should always, always listen to your mother!"

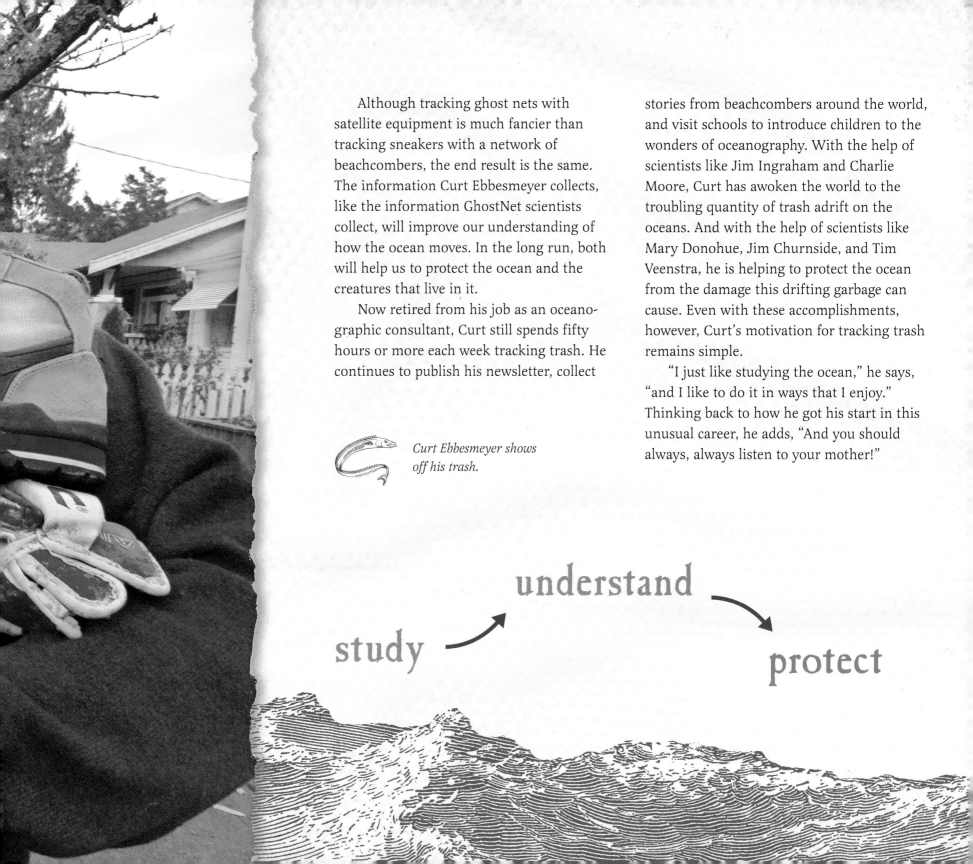

Curt Ebbesmeyer shows off his trash.

study → understand → protect

Glossary

BEACHCOMBER

A person interested in the ocean and its shores and who spends time collecting or observing the natural and man-made items that can be found on beaches.

CLIMATE

The general weather conditions of a geographical region.

CONTAINER SHIP

A ship built for the ocean transport of cargo packed into large containers.

CONVERGENCE ZONE

An oceanic location where multiple surface currents come together and, as a result, force seawater to sink (this sinking process is called downwelling).

CURRENT

A large body of water moving in a certain direction.

DEBRIS

Rubbish or trash; marine debris is rubbish or trash found in or near the ocean.

DEEP OCEAN CURRENTS

Ocean currents that travel far below the surface of the ocean; sometimes called deep sea currents.

DEGREE

A unit of angular distance used to measure longitude and latitude.

DOWNWELLING

Downward movement of oceanic surface waters due to the convergence of currents or to an encounter between currents and coastal landmasses.

EQUATOR

The imaginary line extending around the earth at a point midway between the North Pole and the South Pole and from which latitude is measured.

FLOATS

Name given to floating objects, made mostly of plastic, that oceanographers use in drift experiments.

FLOTSAM

Parts and pieces of a ship found floating on the sea or washed up on a beach.

GHOST NETS

Lost or discarded fishing nets that continue to drift at sea, threatening marine animals and coral reefs.

GYRE

A circular pattern of oceanic surface currents.

HULL

The hollow, lowermost portion of a ship.

ICE FLOES

Large masses of floating ice, as are found in the Arctic Ocean.

JETSAM

Goods or cargo intentionally thrown into the sea and which sink, drift, or wash ashore.

LARVAE

An animal or insect in its immature stages.

LATITUDE

A measure of the distance (in degrees) north or south of the equator.

LONGITUDE

A measure of the distance (in degrees) east or west of the prime meridian.

MERIDIANS

Imaginary lines that circle the planet, converging at the North and South Poles, which are used to measure longitude.

NURDLES

Tiny plastic particles; the term can refer to both plastic pellets produced by the plastic industry or to the degraded bits of larger plastic pieces.

PARALLELS

Imaginary lines that circle the planet in parallel rings between the North Pole and the South Pole and are used to measure latitude.

PLANKTON

Organisms that drift with ocean currents.

PRIME MERIDIAN

An imaginary line that circles the earth, passes through the Royal Observatory at Greenwich, England, and from which we measure longitude.

SURFACE CURRENTS

Ocean currents that circulate the uppermost layers of the sea.

TIDE

The periodic rise and fall of ocean levels all over the planet that results from the differential gravitational pulls of the sun and the moon at these locations at different times.

WAVE

A moving swell formed when energy passes through seawater.

WINDAGE

The extent to which a moving object is deflected by the wind.

WORLD OCEAN

A phrase that refers to the single and continuous body of seawater that covers nearly three quarters of our planet; the world ocean is composed of the Pacific Ocean, the Atlantic Ocean, the Indian Ocean, and the Southern Ocean.

BOOKS TO ENJOY

The Restless Sea
by Carole Garbundy Vogel
(New York: Franklin Watts, 2003)

This six-book series provides an excellent introduction to the ocean, its wildlife, its exploration, its shifting shores, its dangers, its savagery, and its response to human impact.

The Mysterious Ocean Highway
by Deborah Heiligman
(Austin: Steck-Vaughn Company, 2000)

This book provides a historic look at the discovery of surface currents, with particular attention given to the recording by Benjamin Franklin of the Gulf Stream. Readers compare the tools used to study ocean currents in Franklin's day with the tools and techniques of today's oceanographers.

The Kingfisher Young People's Book of Oceans
by David Lambert
(New York: Scholastic, 1998)

This introductory text covers all aspects of "the amazing world above and below the waves."

WEB SITES TO EXPLORE

Beachcombers' and Oceanographers' International Association
www.beachcombers.org
Curt Ebbesmeyer maintains this Web site to keep beachgoers from around the world aware of what he is tracking. Contact him at Curtisebbesmeyer@comcast.net or through his Web site to report interesting beach finds, or to subscribe to his quarterly newsletter, *Beachcombers' Alert!*

Algalita Marine Research Foundation (AMRF)
www.algalita.org
This Web site will acquaint you with the marine conservation organization that sponsored Captain Charles Moore's research. Be sure to visit the Portals to the Sea pages to watch a video of marine life in Long Beach Harbor.

The Ocean Conservancy
www.oceanconservancy.org
This Web site is the place to go if you are interested in tracking trash yourself. The Ocean Conservancy sponsors the International Coastal Cleanup, a worldwide survey and cleanup of beach debris. It also coordinates the National Debris Monitoring Program, an effort to record beach debris nationwide.

The GhostNet Project
www.highseasghost.net
Here you can learn more about the GhostNet Project and track the ghost nets tagged by Captain Moore and his crew.

ACKNOWLEDGMENTS

I extend my heartfelt gratitude to Curt Ebbesmeyer, Jim Ingraham, Charlie Moore, Jim Churnside, Tim Veenstra, and Mary Donohue; this book is a tribute to their passion for understanding and protecting our world ocean. I am grateful to the many others who shared their stories and photographs with me, especially Dean and Tyler Orbison, John Anderson, Steve McLeod, the staff at SEA Lab in Redondo Beach, California, and the crew of the ORV *Alguita*. Special thanks to Dr. Michael Spall and Dr. Philip Richardson of the Woods Hole Oceanographic Institution for their thorough review of the manuscript and to Dr. Eric Luper, Liza Martz, Dawn Lussier, and Gerry Burns for their careful reading of early drafts. It was my great joy to work with my friend Betty Jenewin during this project; her photographs helped make the book complete and her companionship helped keep its author sane. Thanks also to Erica Zappy and to my family for their tireless support of this project. In the words of Curt's father, Paul J. Ebbesmeyer, may the tides be good to you.

> "May the tides be good to you."
>
> — **Paul J. Ebbesmeyer**

PHOTO CREDITS

American Geophysical Union: 15, 16 (Images modified from Ebbesmeyer and Ingraham, Eos 73[34], p. 361, August 25, 1992, with permission of American Geophysical Union)

Gerry Burns: 36

Loree Griffin Burns: 40, 41

Phillip Colla/www.oceanlight.com: iv, 30, 31 (left)

Matt Cramer/AMRF: 37

Jonathan J. Doll, M.Ed.: 3 (top right), 27 (bottom)

Curtis C. Ebbesmeyer: 25

Bernard P. Hanby: 31 (right)

Jan Hinsch/Photo Researchers, Inc.: 29 (top)

W. James Ingraham, Jr.: 13 (bottom right), 32

Laguna Design/Photo Researchers, Inc.: 29 (bottom)

Jody Lemmon, Amphibious Productions/AMRF: 48

NOAA Fisheries: 42, 44, 45

Dean Orbison: 26

Melanie Perry/Greywolf Outdoors Inc.: 38 (right)

Phil Richardson/Bibliotèque Nationale de France: vi

SIO Archives, UCSD: 11

Fatima Sousa: 12

Cynthia Vanderlip: 39

Tim Veenstra/Airborne Technologies, Inc: 46, 47, 49

James White: 5

Don Wilson/Port of Seattle: 6

Pat Wolski and Betty Jenewin: 22

Woods Hole Oceanographic Institution: 13 (middle)

All other photographs by Betty Jenewin

Bibliographic Notes

The best source of information about Curt Ebbesmeyer's work can be found in the *Beachcombers' Alert!* newsletter, which is published four times a year by the Beachcombers' and Oceanographers' International Association (BOIA). You can subscribe by writing to BOIA at 6306 21st Avenue, NE, Seattle, WA 98115-6916. Many magazines and newspapers have printed stories about the sneaker and tub toy spills, including the journal of the American Geophysical Union (*Eos*), *People*, and *Forbes*.

Charles Moore has written an excellent article about his work (*Natural History*, November 2003). Additional information can be found in scientific journals (for example, *Marine Pollution Bulletin*, December 2001), popular magazines (for example, *U.S. News & World Report*, November 4, 2002), and the short documentary *Our Synthetic Sea*. You can purchase this video by writing to Algalita Marine Research Foundation, 148 North Marina Drive, Long Beach, CA 90803.

Readers can learn more about the work of Tim Veenstra and Jim Churnside and the GhostNet project at their Web site, www.highseasghost.net. Mary Donohue's net debris survey work has been published in scientific journals (for example, *Marine Pollution Bulletin*, December 2001) and discussed in lay publications (for example, *Makai Quarterly*, Spring 2003).

Dr. Ebbesmeyer gives a presentation about surface currents in the Pacific Ocean.

Index

Page numbers in *italics* refer to photographs.